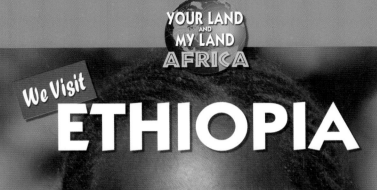

YOUR LAND
AND
MY LAND
AFRICA

We Visit

ETHIOPIA

John
Bankston

Mitchell Lane
PUBLISHERS

P.O. Box 196
Hockessin, Delaware 19707

YOUR LAND
AND
MY LAND
AFRICA

Egypt
Ethiopia
Ghana
Kenya
Libya
Madagascar
Morocco
Nigeria
Rwanda
South Africa

IBYA

EGYPT

Aswān

YOUR LAND
AND
MY LAND
AFRICA

We Visit

ETHIOPIA

SUDAN

ulf of Ader

Addis
Ababa

Mitchell Lane
PUBLISHERS

Printing   1   2   3   4   5   6   7   8   9

Library of Congress Cataloging-in-Publication
Bankston, John, 1974-
 We visit Ethiopia / by John Bankston.
    p. cm. — (Your land and my land. Africa)
 Includes bibliographical references and index.
 ISBN 978-1-61228-302-9 (library bound)
1. Ethiopia—Juvenile literature. I. Title. II. Series: Your land and my land (Mitchell Lane Publishers). Africa.
 DT373.B24 2013
 963—dc23
                                                              2012009475

eBook ISBN: 9781612283760

PUBLISHER'S NOTE: This story is based on the author's extensive research, which he believes to be accurate. Documentation of this research is on page 61.

    The internet sites referenced herein were active as of the publication date. Due to the fleeting nature of some websites, we cannot guarantee they will all be active when you are reading this book.

                                                              PLB

Contents

Introduction

A generation ago, Ethiopia was in the news for all the wrong reasons. In the early 1980s, the country endured drought and ongoing civil war. Hundreds of thousands of its citizens faced starvation. In the United States, their faces filled television screens across the country as nightly newscasts highlighted their plight. In December of 1984, Irish musician Bob Geldof's "Band Aid" project raised nearly twenty million dollars through sales of a single, "Do They Know It's Christmas?" performed by a number of well-known musicians including Phil Collins and U2's Bono. The next summer, "Live Aid" concerts raised over 200 million dollars.

Nearly thirty years later, famine is all many people think of when Ethiopia is mentioned. Yet it is so much more. Located in the sub-Saharan portion of Africa (south of the Sahara Desert), Ethiopia rests on the Horn of Africa, a triangular land mass that juts out from the rest of the continent like a sharp tooth. It is also one of the most mountainous countries on the continent. These mountains protected the country from invasion, but at the same time, isolated its people. Within its borders they developed a distinct culture, one radically different from the cultures of its neighbors.

Near the city of Gondar, fields and farmland are plentiful.

ETHIOPIA

AFRICA

And while many residents worry about getting enough to eat, Ethiopia is also a country of tremendous beauty and fantastic advantages. A small bowl of its locally grown grain, teff, can provide enough energy for the entire day. Its Central Highlands area, while densely populated, offers mild weather and a lengthy growing season.

Today Africa is home to fifty-seven independent countries. Their borders often change, as they did in 1993 when the northern portion of Ethiopia split off to form Eritrea. This division left the country without a seaport—a challenge because it is dependent on money from exports like coffee.

Bordered on the north by Djibouti, Eritrea, and Sudan; on the west by South Sudan; on the south by Kenya; and on the east by Somalia, Ethiopia's history goes back thousands of years. One of its rulers, the Queen of Sheba, is mentioned in the Bible. According to Ethiopian legend, she had a son with King Solomon in the 10th century B.C.E. That son became the first ruler in the Solomonic dynasty—a monarchy which lasted thousands of years until well into the 20th century C.E.

Despite its hot, dry climate, a variety of animals thrive in the Great Rift Valley, including zebras.

An Isolated World

Welcome to Ethiopia. You might be surprised to know that out of all the countries in Africa, Ethiopia is the only one that has remained independent throughout its history. With the exception of a five-year occupation by Italy in the time leading up to and during World War II, the country has always been in charge of its own destiny. Although Italian forces didn't stay long and didn't travel past Ethiopia's largest cities, their unsuccessful attempt at colonization left its mark. Over seventy years later, most Ethiopian restaurants serve spaghetti and even rural communities have espresso machines for Italian coffees like cappuccino. The country's citizens still say *ciao,* Italian for "goodbye."

Over the last thousand years, Ethiopia has adopted elements from many cultures. Arab traders and European explorers made their marks. Yet the country did not endure the invasions, occupations, and colonizations affecting its neighbors. Geography played a huge role. The Central Highlands, the area with the most people, was sheltered by rugged mountain ranges and deserts on all sides. Even the seaport Ethiopia once controlled was a long, difficult journey from its former capital.

Visitors expecting the dry savannas of neighboring Kenya or the parched deserts of nearby Sudan are often surprised by Ethiopia's landscape. Although large sections of the country are indeed as dry as the Sahara, its rainforests receive many feet of rainfall every year.

Slicing the country in two from northeast to southwest, the Great Rift Valley (or East African Rift) is a reminder of the powerful forces working beneath the earth's surface. Africa itself is being slowly pulled apart by the separation of tectonic plates. In several million years, the continent will be split in two.

These dividing forces are the same forces which created the country's mountains about 20 to 30 million years ago. At that time, a plume of white hot matter some 1,200 miles (1,930 kilometers) across pushed its way up across the Afar Region of Ethiopia. A large dome formed; it later split apart to form the Gulf of Aden, the Red Sea, and the Great Rift Valley. Volcanoes erupted continuously—until they had covered the region with enough volcanic rock to bury the entire United States under 60 feet (18 meters) of it.[1]

When the volcanoes more or less ceased their activity, they left behind an isolated country—and one of the most breathtaking geological oddities on earth. Today, the Great Rift Valley is a deep trench with its lowest point—the Afar Depression—some 394 feet (120 meters) below sea level. With an unrelenting sun shining down, and blocked from any breezes by the sides of the rift, the area experiences some of the hottest temperatures on the planet. Daytime highs can reach 145°F (63°C).

To the east of the Great Rift Valley lies the Somali Plateau. Here is the rocky semi-desert of Ethiopia which reaches all the way to the Ogaden Plateau and the entire southeastern portion of the country. To

FYI FACT:

Born in 1932 near the town of Mendida, Abebe Bikila came from humble beginnings. As an adult, he became a security guard for the Ethiopian Emperor Haile Selassie to earn money, but soon began training for marathons in his free time. At the 1960 Olympics in Rome, Bikila was added to the Ethiopian team at the last minute to fill in for an injured team member. Shoes were supposed to be supplied by Adidas, but there were none left that fit him. So, he ran the marathon barefoot. Not only did he win the gold medal, making him the first black African to do so, but his time also set an Olympic record.

WHERE IN THE WORLD IS ETHIOPIA?

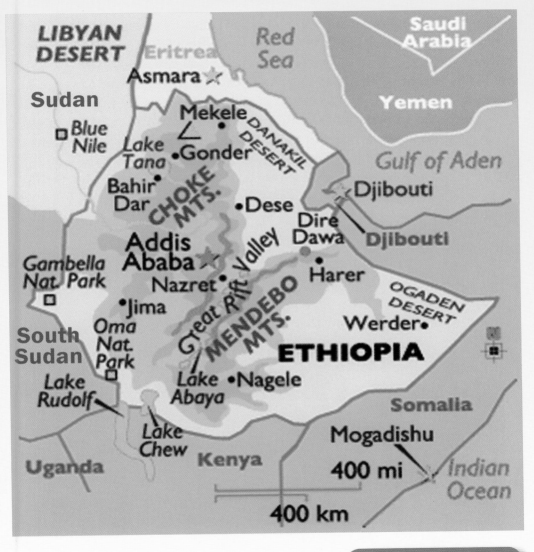

LIBYAN DESERT

Eritrea

Red Sea

Saudi Arabia

Asmara ☆

Sudan

Yemen

Blue Nile

Mekele

DANAKIL DESERT

Gulf of Aden

Lake Tana

Gonder

Bahir Dar

CHOKE MTS.

Dese

Dire Dawa

Djibouti

Djibouti

Addis Ababa ☆

Great Rift Valley

Harer

OGADEN DESERT

Gambella Nat. Park

Nazret

MENDEBO MTS.

Werder

South Sudan

Oma Nat. Park

Jima

ETHIOPIA

Lake Rudolf

Lake Abaya

Nagele

Somalia

Lake Chew

Kenya

Mogadishu

Uganda

400 mi

Indian Ocean

400 km

Where in the World ◎

the west of the Great Rift Valley is the Ethiopian Plateau, where most of the land ranges in altitude from 4,900 to 9,800 feet (1,500 to 3,000 meters). The high altitude produces cold nights, while its proximity to the equator means it also has very hot days. In some parts of the plateau, it can feel like both winter and summer in just twenty-four hours.

The height of this plateau means oxygen levels are far lower than at sea level. Some of the best runners on the planet grow up here. Accustomed to breathing the thin air, they perform even better in the oxygen-rich environments of most athletic competitions. Only Kenya produces more world champions—runners there breathe the equally thin air of the Mount Kenya region.

Runners who train along the Ethiopian Plateau are only bested by Kenyans who live around Mount Kenya, shown here.

ETHIOPIA FACTS AT A GLANCE

Ethiopian flag

Full name: Federal Democratic Republic of Ethiopia

Languages: Oromigna (official regional) 33.8%, Amharic (also Amarigna; official) 29.3%, Somaligna 6.2%, Tigrigna (official regional) 5.9%, Sidamigna 4%, Wolayitigna 2.2%, Guaragigna 2%, Hadiyigna 1.7%, Affarigna 1.7%, Gamogna 1.5%, other 11.7%, English (official; major foreign language taught in schools), Arabic (official)

Population: 91,195,675 (July 2012 est.)

Land area: 386,102 square miles (1,000,000 square kilometers); almost twice the size of Texas

Capital: Addis Ababa

Government: Federal Republic

Ethnic makeup: Oromo 34.5%, Amhara 26.9%, Somali 6.2%, Tigray 6.1%, Sidama 4%, Gurage 2.5%, Welayta 2.3%, Hadiya 1.7%, Afar 1.7%, Gamo 1.5%, Gedeo 1.3%, other 11.3%

Religions: Orthodox Christian 43.5%, Muslim 33.9%, Protestant 18.6%, traditional 2.6%, Catholic 0.7%, other 0.7%

Exports: coffee, khat, gold, leather products, live animals, oilseed

Imports: food and live animals, petroleum and petroleum products, chemicals, machinery, motor vehicles, cereals, textiles

Crops: cereals, pulses, coffee, oilseed, cotton, sugarcane, potatoes, khat, cut flowers

Average high temperatures: Addis Ababa: March 77°F (25°C), August 70°F (21°C)

Average annual rainfall: Addis Ababa: 48.7 inches (123.6 centimeters)

Highest point: Ras Dashen Mountain—14,928 feet (4,550 meters)

Longest river: Awash River—750 miles (1,200 kilometers)

Flag: Three equal horizontal bands of green (top), yellow, and red, with a yellow pentagram and single yellow rays emanating from the angles between the points on a light blue disk centered on the three bands; green represents hope and the fertility of the land, yellow symbolizes justice and harmony, while red stands for sacrifice and heroism in the defense of the land; the blue of the disk symbolizes peace and the pentagram represents the unity and equality of the nationalities and peoples of Ethiopia.

National anthem: "Whedefit Gesgeshi Woud Enat Ethiopia" (March Forward, Dear Mother Ethiopia)

National sports: No official national sport, but football (soccer) and competitive running are popular.

National flower: Calla lily

National animal: Abyssinian Lion

Source: *CIA World Factbook:* Ethiopia

Semien Mountains

Half of the land above 6,500 feet (1,980 meters) on the African continent is in Ethiopia. Nearly 80 percent of Africa's land over 9,800 feet (2,990 meters) is in Ethiopia.[2] The country's tallest mountain is Ras Dashen, located in the Semien Mountains of northern Ethiopia. At 14,928 feet (4,550 meters), it stands as one of the highest mountains on the continent.

Mountains not only isolated the people of Ethiopia, they isolated the animals as well. Because many animals that developed here never traveled beyond the mountain borders, the country boasts a number of unique species. Some forty-two species of mammals and twenty-three species of birds are found only in Ethiopia. Malcolm's Ethiopia toad is a prime example of a creature that has adapted to its environment. Surviving in areas between 10,500 and 13,100 feet (3,200 and 4,000 meters) above sea level, its eggs develop in the cold, damp soil found in this environment. The walia ibex, a hearty goat whose sharp horns sweep back over its shoulders, also thrives in high altitudes. One of the rarest mammals in Ethiopia, it enjoys the craggy cliffs along the Semien Mountain range on the northern plateau. Even rarer along these mountains, the Ethiopian wolf (also called the Semien fox) is the most threatened wolf in the world. Approximately 500 survive in the wild, many under the protection of Ethiopia's Bale Mountains National Park.

Many consider the gelada baboon the most amusing of Ethiopia's native species. These altitude-tolerant primates are comfortable breathing the thin air of the Semien Range where they make their homes. Although not true baboons (they are the last surviving species of grass-grazing primates), they look like baboons with their pinched, ancient looking faces, and wild tufts of hair growing from their heads. Nature's couch potatoes, they have adapted to the scarce food supply by eating all day and moving as little as possible. Surviving on a diet of grass and other vegetation, the female cannot hide her true feelings. When she sees a male she likes, a patch of hairless skin on her chest turns red!

Mountains and deserts are challenging environments for people. The more hospitable Central Highlands offer ideal temperatures and a moist climate. In the cool season, it is usually no colder than 41°F (5°C), while the warmest daytime highs rarely exceed 79°F (26°C). This is part of the reason for the area's dense population. The capital city of Addis Ababa is home to almost three million people. With a size of around 204 square miles (528 square kilometers), it has 14,000 people per square mile (5,400 people per square kilometer). (By comparison, New York City has some 27,500 people per square mile, or 10,600 people per square kilometer).

Beyond its cities, the Central Highlands are dotted with farmland. This is where foods like teff, the ensete (sometimes called the false banana), and the Oromo potato are grown. Coffee, a main Ethiopian export, is also grown in the Central Highlands. The Highlands contain more native plants that can be used as food than any other area in Africa.[3]

Despite facing enormous challenges throughout the country's history, Ethiopians have endured for thousands of years. Most scientists believe modern humans can trace their background to primitive prehumans called hominids. These apelike creatures flourished, eventually crossing land bridges into Asia and Europe before migrating across the planet. Their journey began in the Great Rift Valley, one or two million years after they first stood upright.

Millions of years ago the Afar Region was a fertile landscape that was home to human ancestors; today it is a hot and nearly lifeless desert.

Chapter 2

Beginnings

Emerald leaves stretched to the sky. Enormous trees nearly blotted out the sun. Dense foliage cast shadows upon thick brush below. Millions of years ago, the Afar Region was a lush forest. Today, much of it is a hot and nearly lifeless desert.

Close to four million years ago, a creature many consider one of humankind's earliest relatives struggled to survive. It lived in both trees and on the ground; its teeth were not sharp like the teeth of meat eaters, so it survived by eating whatever it could find including leaves, fruit, seeds, and the occasional lizard. Lethal carnivores like raptors, saber-toothed cats, and hyenas stalked it and other small primates.

Closely related to the ape, it was covered in fur and stumpy looking, with short legs and long, lanky arms. It had a thick ridge over its brow and a brain less than one-third the size of modern man's. This was *Australopithecus afarensis*. Scientists classify this creature as a hominid —an upright-standing primate mammal. This category includes modern humans.

In 1974, in the present-day Afar Region, close to the Ethiopian town of Hadar, the first *Australopithecus afarensis* and one of the oldest skeletons of a pre-human was discovered. It was a fossil—the petrified, stone-like remains of a young female who lived and died in an area once containing a lake or a marsh. The fossil was over three million years old. In life, she was less than 4 feet (1.2 meters) tall. Despite ape-like features, her legs allowed her to stand upright and even walk for short distances. Called *Dinknesh* in Ethiopia for "she is wonderful," in the United States, she is known simply as "Lucy."

Australopithecus afarensis lived on earth for approximately 900,000 years. During this period of time it adapted to its environment by changing—evolving. Eventually these changes produced a new species, *Australopithecus aethiopicus,* which had a larger brain and sharper teeth. The *Australopithecus aethiopicus* thrived in southern Ethiopia's Omo Valley some 2.5 million years ago.

In 1994, even older pre-human fossils were discovered. Around the modern village of Aramis, which lies along the Awash River, 4.4 million-year-old fossils were discovered. Those fossils together with Lucy "appear to confirm the estimates of molecular biologists engaged in genetic research that the divergence between man and the modern apes occurred some four to six million years ago."[1]

In other words, scientists believe these fossils provide evidence supporting an important theory: millions of years ago, some apes continued to evolve as apes while others evolved into people. The ape who first stood upright, is sometimes called the "missing link," because no fossils have been found to prove its existence. Today many scientists dismiss the need to discover the missing link. Others consider its absence proof that evolution either never occurred or did not occur as described.

In 1996, 50 miles (80 kilometers) north of Aramis (and about 180 miles—290 kilometers—northeast of the capital), an archaeological dig unearthed ancient tools. Digging in the area surrounding the Gona River in the Afar Depression revealed that the excavated section was composed of volcanic tuff. This compressed volcanic ash formed rocks that were scattered across the landscape by a volcanic eruption. The eruption took place about 2.5 million years ago; stone tools encased in the tuff were estimated to be from around the same time period. These tools discovered in Ethiopia were at least 600,000 years older than similar ones uncovered in Tanzania.

The development of tools was a major milestone in human evolution. Soon after tools were first used on earth, a new species appeared: *Homo habilis.* Smarter and comfortable on their two legs, they mastered the use of hand axes and knives. Crafted from stone, these tools helped *Homo habilis* cut up their food.

Scientists believe the ancestors of all modern humans originated in Kenya, Tanzania, and the Omo Valley region of Ethiopia. A more recent relative, *Homo erectus* (or "upright man"), used the natural land bridges that once existed to cross into Asia and Europe. About the same size and shape as modern humans, they could walk and even run long distances. Unlike earlier ancestors, *Homo erectus* did not live in trees. Their tools were sharp and well-crafted. They killed large animals and ate well. By around 750,000 years ago, they were able to cook their food. At that time, they harnessed a vital tool for their success on planet Earth: fire.

Fire did more than heat food. It provided warmth as *Homo erectus* spread into regions with harsher winters than eastern Africa. It also marked their superiority to other animals—animals who feared fire, instead of using it.

These primates continued to evolve. Eventually, about 200,000 years ago the first *Homo sapiens* (Latin for "wise man") appeared. Commonly called human beings, *Homo sapiens* first appeared in Ethiopia's Dire Dawa Region and the upper Awash valley over 70,000 years ago. They spread into the foothills of Ethiopia's Central Highlands, interacting with other early settlers along the Nile River.

Descendants of these early humans developed a unique country. Once called Abyssinia, Ethiopia is a country protected by mountains, a place with its own way of life. Witnessing Ethiopia's history can be done without visiting a museum; many of the country's different ethnic groups continue to practice the centuries-old traditions of their ancestors today.

Wearing paint instead of clothing, members of the tribes that inhabit the Omo Valley live much as they have for thousands of years.

Culture

The remains of humankind's early ancestors were discovered not far from the home of the Mursi tribe. Along the southwestern tip of Ethiopia, in the Omo Valley, tribespeople blend with the surrounding landscape. Atop their heads, ornaments made of leaves, flowers, feathers, or tree branches provide shade from the relentless sun. Above bare feet, their shins are protected by zebu skin—from a type of cattle they raise. For many, the rest of their bodies are covered not in clothing or even animal hides, but paint.

In an area where the daytime highs often top 100°F (38°C), it makes sense to substitute paint for clothes. Paints are produced from clay and other natural materials found in the Great Rift Valley. The Mursi decorate themselves in bright reds and vivid greens, dark yellows and whites. They don't use mirrors. Instead they rely upon a creative instinct honed for hundreds of years as they paint themselves or one another.

Alongside the Karo, the Bodi, the Tsamai, and the Suri (who frequently interact with the Mursi, and share their talents for decoration and body painting), the Mursi are one of dozens of tribes inhabiting the lower Omo Valley in southwest Ethiopia and northern Kenya. Today, they survive as all ancient people survived before farms or ranches, before food was produced or raised. They are nomadic, moving from place to place without a fixed home.

"The decorative focus on the body... is strongly connected with nomadic lifestyles," explains photographer Hans Silvester. "The body is seen almost as a piece of territory, with skin and flesh replacing the stone, ceramics and textiles typical of other cultures. Nomads always have the ability to leave everything behind and travel."[1]

Yet this ancient tribe, their naked skin dressed in the brilliant colors of the terrain, remains connected to the 21ˢᵗ century. Their necklaces often include the discarded tops of ballpoint pens and empty rifle cartridges alongside traditional shells and beads. Male or female, their heads are carefully shaved. Today, tribe members use razor blades from India or sharpened springs from Range Rovers.

Even in the depths of undeveloped wilderness, the horrors of modern warfare have touched the tribe—as they have touched many others in Ethiopia. This is the country's reality. Ethiopians inhabit two worlds—the traditional and the modern. Its cities offer internet connections and cell phones, but in rural areas farmers rely on oxen and women use nonelectric treadle sewing machines.

Still, on a continent where ongoing culture clashes predate written language, Ethiopia's different ethnic groups coexist with few conflicts. Since 1994, the country has been divided into nine regions, each one created for a different ethnic group. For example, the Tigray Region

A field of sunflowers blooms in the Tigray Region.

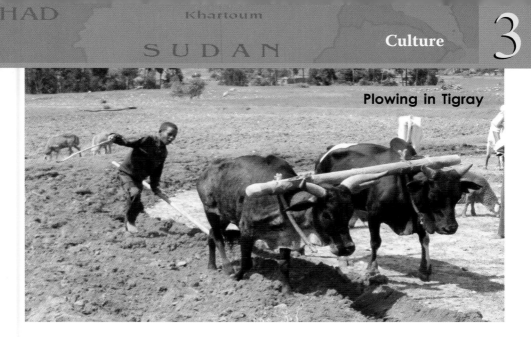

Plowing in Tigray

(previously Region One) is the home of the Tigray tribe—and in that portion of the country they are the dominant group and make the decisions affecting the region. This group, primarily Orthodox Christian, herds sheep, cattle, and goats. They still use the *maresha,* a primitive plow powered by two oxen restrained by a wooden yoke.

While members of the Gurage merchant tribe are spread throughout the country, they have been assigned to the Southern Nations, Nationalities, and People's Region. Still, with over seventy different tribes, providing representation for all of Ethiopia's ethnic groups is a challenge.

There are small tribes, like the Omo Valley's tiny Karo tribe, numbering only 1,500 members. The Oromo, on the other hand, is the largest group, representing approximately one out of every three Ethio-

FYI FACT:

From coin collections to displays of traditional medicine and burial customs, Ethiopia's Ethnological Museum offers visitors a variety of exhibits showcasing the country's traditions, cultures, and history. Located in Addis Ababa, the museum was once a palace belonging to the nation's last emperor, Haile Selassie. Today, tourists can see Selassie's bathroom and bedroom.

Dressed in traditional garb, these Oromo women belong to the largest ethnic group in Ethiopia.

pians. They moved into the central and western parts of Ethiopia in the 1500s as pastoralists—nomads who raised livestock. Originating in the south of the country, today they inhabit much of Ethiopia.

The Oromo are the dominant group in Ethiopia, but numerous other tribes make up the complete country. Some live the way their ancestors have for centuries, others embrace the modern world. The languages which dominate this part of East Africa have been developed over thousands of years.

By 800 to 500 B.C.E., civilizations had arisen on the highlands of Eritrea and Tigray. Their writing resembled the South Arabian script, which in Ethiopia developed into Ge'ez script. Originally used to write the Ge'ez language, today the script is used for many of Ethiopia's languages, including Amharic and Tigrigna. The Ge'ez language is one of the oldest written languages in the world; it is still spoken in Ethiopia, although primarily in religious services.

Ethnic identity is not just about the way a group dresses. It also includes the way they interact with each other and how they help other members of their tribe. One of the best examples of this is *debo.* Some call it the country's largest social welfare program, but it is not govern-

Debo is often used to develop small farms, like this one.

ment run. Instead debo is a traditional method of coming to the aid of those in need.

When a farmer is unable to work, or the work he needs to have done is too large to complete on his own, he asks his neighbors for help. At a scheduled time they come by to help him with his land. In exchange, the farmer promises to work on their farms when they need help.

Debo is similar to Amish farmers pitching in together to raise a barn or the way the charitable organization Habitat for Humanity requires those who receive their houses to work building homes for others. Debo is an age-old practice handed down from generation to generation. Other traditions can be seen not only in the ways the people dress or speak, but in how they prepare a meal when a visitor sits down to dinner.

The Merkato is the largest outdoor market in Africa. It opened in 1935, soon after Italy invaded Ethiopia.

On the Table

Stretching across the Addis Ketema district in Ethiopia's capital city, the Merkato or "new market," offers unique wares for visitor and native alike. This open-air shopping center thrives in the Central Highlands area's generally pleasant weather.

The Merkato is the largest outdoor market in Africa. After the occupying Italians made the popular St. George's Market forbidden to Ethiopians, locals opened the Merkato half-a-mile (0.8 kilometers) west. Today, St. George's Market offers upscale goods and caters to tourists. The Merkato, on the other hand, operates much like a seaport. Goods arrive from all over, while merchandise is purchased by people who live within walking distance as well as visitors who make their homes in towns and cities across the globe.

Home to over 7,000 different businesses, including 2,500 retail stores and employing more than 13,000 people, the market is a bustle of activity. Crowded with men, women, children, and even animals, it is common for foreigners to be charged more than natives for the same item. Unlike the goods in American stores, few items have price tags. Shoppers are expected to haggle. T-shirts and handcrafted wood sculptures are bought by tourists just steps from where native women in traditional clothing bargain for spices.

Coffee seller John Bolton describes the Merkato as "a huge setting where they sell everything imaginable... everything was carried in to sell, and often times it had to be carried for several blocks. I witnessed many ten year olds carrying baskets on their heads laden with melons or tomatoes. These baskets easily weighed twice as much as their porters."[1]

Sellers at the Merkato offer everything from household goods to colorful clothes. In a country where most live on a few dollars a day, "repair not replace" is a way of life. A large selection of nonelectric treadle sewing machines are for sale to anyone who hopes to produce their own clothing or just fix a tear. Quite similar to the ones invented over 150 years ago, these machines are operated by foot pedals.

Yet in the controlled chaos of the bustling market, it is not the goods that most visitors notice. It is the food.

Enormous bags of teff, the local grain, are piled up not far from stands holding everything from bananas and grapes to red onions and blocks of butter. Meats are on display while nearby, women seated in front of scales measure out the ingredients for a traditional stew.

Visitors sampling Ethiopian food generally agree with the country's reputation for having the spiciest food on the continent. Spices do more than enhance the flavor. They also keep the meat from going bad. In a country where many lack electricity or refrigerators, spices remain a vital preservative.

The most popular additive is a spice blend made with over a dozen different spices. *Berbere* (or *awaze,* in paste form) is so important that in traditional households, women who make the best berbere are said to have the best chance of landing a husband.

Wat, considered Ethiopia's national dish, is a stew prepared with a variety of meats—including lamb, chicken, or beef. It is never made with pork because the adherents of the country's dominant religions —Orthodox Christianity, Islam, and Judaism—are not allowed to eat it. In fact, pork is almost impossible to find in Ethiopia.

Wat is extremely spicy—traditional recipes call for a tablespoon of berbere for each serving. Served in a large bowl, wat usually makes up the main course. Besides wat, a meal might include *dabo kolo,* a fried snack served before the main course, *iab,* a cheese similar to

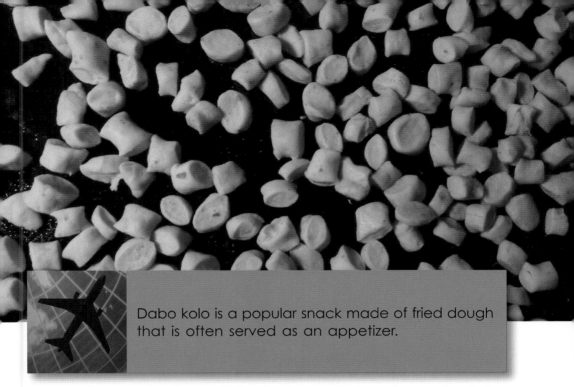

Dabo kolo is a popular snack made of fried dough that is often served as an appetizer.

cottage cheese, and *tej,* a traditional wine made from honey that helps wash down all the spicy food.

All of the food, including the wat, is served communally. Everyone eats from the same plate. In Ethiopia, all food is "finger food." There are no forks or spoons. Instead, everyone uses their hands to pick up their meal. Before the first dish is even served, everyone washes their hands.

In a traditional home, guests sit on a low couch in front of a wicker table that is brought to them. The rest of the diners surround the table, sitting on low stools that are less than a foot high and covered with monkey fur. The woman of the house then brings out a copper pitcher and a basin. Pouring warm water from the pitcher over the guest's right hand, she then offers a towel hanging from her arm that the guest can use. This elaborate ritual actually has its roots in religious ceremony, not hygiene.

After the hand washing is complete, the entire table—called a *mesab*—is removed. Returned a few minutes later with a domed cover, the dining options for the evening are unveiled when the cover is lifted.

The jebena

The entire meal is served on *injera*. Like most food served in Ethiopia, it is prepared as it has been for hundreds of years. Injera's main ingredient remains vital for the future of Ethiopia.

Injera bread is made with teff, a grain that is native to Ethiopia. It has been grown in the country for thousands of years, perhaps originating as far back as 6,000 years ago. Although the grain is the size of a pinhead, author John Reader explains, "size is no measure of quality. In its value as a human food, teff is superior to any other cereal grown in Ethiopia... A single daily portion of teff supplies enough... essential amino acids to sustain life without any other source of protein, while two daily portions are enough to ensure good health."[2]

The injera is used as a covering for the table like a tablecloth. But this tablecloth is eaten. Pieces of the injera are torn off, and the food is rolled up inside the bread. Dessert is just as unusual. Instead of a sweet treat, cheese or raw ground beef is served along with coffee, which is prepared ceremonially. After the coffee beans are roasted and ground, the powder is placed in a pot or a *jebena* with boiling water. Coffee is then served in tiny cups; usually each person enjoys two or three of them. Burning incense and the washing of hands ends the meal.

What an Ethiopian eats is determined both by their religion and by what's available. Although meat is an important ingredient in many traditional Ethiopian meals, few traditional Ethiopians eat meat every

The very first coffee tree—Arabica—was harvested in Ethiopia. Growing to a height of 30 to 40 feet (9 to 12 meters), the coffee tree sprouts berries which are picked when ripe. Each berry contains two beans. Over a thousand years ago, Ethiopians ate these beans or made them into a wine. Around 1,000 C.E., the bean was brewed into the familiar coffee beverage in Arabia. Some six hundred years later, Ethiopian coffee beans were brought to Europe, and Arabica trees were planted soon after. Trees from Paris provided the seeds for coffee trees planted in South America and the Caribbean. Today, Arabica beans are the source of more than 70 percent of the world's coffee.

day. Orthodox Tewahedo Christians make up Ethiopia's largest religious group. Their faith demands periods of fasting—when no food is eaten—and other times, like Wednesdays and Fridays, when no meat or dairy (like butter, cheese, and milk) is allowed. Muslims make up a significant part of the population; their religion also has periods of fasting. When meat is not part of the meal, a vegetable stew called *alecha* is one option. Although it does not contain berbere, it offers both red and green peppers along with onions. No matter what the occasion, most Ethiopians avoid bland meals.

Although alecha is often eaten during times when meat is prohibited, religion is not the only reason meats are not consumed. Like many sub-Saharan countries, only a small portion of Ethiopia's land supports farming. Today many of its citizens face starvation and nearly half the country's population is considered undernourished—they simply don't get enough to eat. The country is growing at an incredible rate; until the late 1990s, the average Ethiopian woman gave birth to nearly seven children. According to the United Nations Population Division, the country's population is on track to nearly double from 91 million in 2012 to 174 million in 2050. The U.S. Census Bureau expects Ethiopia's population to grow even faster, tripling to 278 million by 2050.[3] As one of the three fastest-growing countries in Africa (along with Tanzania and Nigeria), Ethiopia's future is dependent on the same factors that helped bring down a powerful empire over 1,500 years ago. That empire's success, like modern Ethiopia's, began with the region's herders and farmers.

Ancient Ethiopians traded raw goods like gold, ivory, and myrrh, for finished products like cloth.

Trades

Today buying a pack of gum at the supermarket requires money. So does buying a computer online. It doesn't matter if the purchase is made using an online payment system, cash or check, credit, or debit card. The transaction requires money. While in the United States, items are priced in U.S. dollars, the Ethiopian birr is the currency used in Ethiopia.

The word "trade" is often used today. But modern phrases like "foreign trade" or "trading partners" rely on a word born from an ancient practice. Before money was used, goods were not purchased but traded for other goods. For example, ivory was plentiful in ancient Ethiopia, because elephants once were. Salt was rare there, and difficult to transport. Often ivory was *traded* for salt. Ethiopia became powerful partly because the region was home to ivory, gold, and other goods which were both rare and desired elsewhere.

Egyptians traded with Ethiopians for incense collected from resin-bearing trees. Myrrh, for example, was used in the Egyptians' elaborate burial ceremonies to help prevent the decay of dead bodies. Some Egyptian tombs depict Ethiopians piloting flat, raft-like boats with sails.

Ancient Ethiopians traded raw goods—like rhino horns, ivory, gold, and silver—for finished products like cloth, tools, metal, and jewelry.

Around 3000 B.C.E., Egyptians trading with Ethiopians living along the borderlands of Sudan called the land Punt. South Arabian inscriptions written in the old Ethiopian language of Ge'ez referred to the people of this country as Habashat or Habesha. Until the 1900s, Eu-

FYI FACT:

Today the illegal trade of rhino horn and ivory continues. The slaughter of elephants, rhinos, and other animals for body parts considered sacred or rare in places like China has led to their near-extinction. Over the last few years, as many in China have become rich, the demand for ivory has greatly increased. It is now worth as much as $900 USD per pound. Although elephants once roamed freely around parts of Ethiopia, their numbers have dwindled drastically. Today they survive in a small portion of the southwest and in protected parks. Across Africa, elephants number over 400,000 but the International Fund for Animal Welfare estimates some 36,000 are killed every year.[1]

ropeans called the country Abyssinia. Ethiopia, a Greek phrase meaning "burned faces" was in use by around the 8th century B.C.E. to describe the Kush region, or even most of explored Africa. Eventually, it was used to describe the country. In the 4th century C.E., the word was first used by King Ezana when he wrote an inscription calling his empire both "Habashat" and "Ethiopia."

Inhabited for thousands of years, Ethiopia has been known by many different names. Its first settlements were campsites built by nomads who realized the animals they hunted were plentiful in different locations at certain times of the year.

When people began raising livestock like sheep and cattle around 9,000 years ago, they remained nomadic. Known as pastoralists, they were constantly moving as they sought food for their animals. Many people in Africa still live this way. Today the open plains they have relied upon for centuries are being developed for homes and businesses, or privately owned farmland.

While pastoralists roamed, others raised their animals on fixed plots of land and grew domestic versions of wild grains. Societies grew and prospered partly because instead of small, related groups of hunter-gatherers, villagers were not as dependent on each other. They also possessed different skills—not everyone was a farmer or herder.

By 7000 B.C.E., they raised cattle, sheep, goats, and donkeys; 4,000 years later, early Ethiopians were cultivating some thirty-six different crops. But beginning around 5000 B.C.E., Ethiopians who'd made their homes in low-lying areas to the west were increasingly impacted by a warmer and dryer environment. It was worse than enduring a season or two of dry weather. Instead, the area's climate changed. Today climate change is often linked to human activity. Some 7,000 years ago, the climate changed without gas-burning engines or polluting factories. Instead, an area once supporting thousands became a barren desert naturally. Today, the western lowlands are a desolate area running north-south along the country's border with Sudan. Even the lower valleys of the Blue Nile, Baro, and Setit Rivers are home to very few people.

Those who could fled. They built new homes in the Central Highlands. Abundant rainfall and rich soil allowed them to prosper. Their descendants entered history, but accounts of life in Ethiopia from before 100 B.C.E. come from outsiders.

Central Highlands

The Queen of Sheba

One Ethiopian ruler was included in the most widely read book in history. Her name was the Queen of Sheba (or Queen Makeda in Ethiopia). Her inclusion in the Bible made her known across the world. As described in First Kings: "Now when the queen of Sheba heard about the fame of Solomon... she came to test him with difficult questions. So she came to Jerusalem with a very large retinue, with camels carrying spices and very much gold and precious stones. When she came to Solomon, she spoke with him about all that was in her heart. Solomon answered all her questions; nothing was hidden from the king which he did not explain to her..." Solomon, according to verse thirteen, gave her "all her desire which she requested."[2]

Ethiopian legend says that she left Israel with more than just presents. The country's national epic is called the *Kebra Nagast* or *"The Glory of Kings."* The stories within were widely told centuries before it was published over 700 years ago. One of the most significant tales claims Sheba had a son whom she named Menelik. His father was King Solomon.

Arriving in Jerusalem as an adult, he met his father. According to the *Kebra Nagast,* when he returned to Ethiopia, he brought with him the Ark of the Covenant. This sacred vessel contained fragments from the original Ten Commandments. Whether it was given to him as a gift by Solomon or Menelik stole it, Ethiopia's Orthodox Church says that it remains in Ethiopia today. Every church has a copy of the Ark, called a *tabot.*

The tabot is displayed during the early morning hours of Timkat on January 19. Timkat (known elsewhere in the world as Epiphany) celebrates the baptism of Jesus. At around 2 a.m., congregants attend services near their closest body of water. The Ethiopian faithful gather to see their church's copy of the tabot brought down. The water is blessed, and some of the members of the church immerse themselves in the water to renew their baptismal vows. To worshippers, the church on its own is just a building; it is the tabot which makes the building holy.

Today the Central Highlands contain more indigenous plants that can be used as food than any other region in Africa. Cultivated on the Highlands' plateau was a grain ideally suited for the region, one that thrived where others failed. This was teff. According to John Reader, it "fueled the growth of a civilization whose size and sophistication was unmatched in sub-Saharan Africa."[3]

This kingdom is often overlooked; it is not as well-known as the Greek, Roman, or Egyptian empires. Nevertheless the Aksum (or Axum) Empire in its time was as powerful and famous as its better-known rivals. The area around the capital city of Aksum had been inhabited for thousands of years; around 100 B.C.E. it became a primary center of trade. Persian leaders considered it the equal of their own country along with Rome and perhaps China.

The empire included the highlands of modern-day Eritrea and Tigray. From the port city of Adulis, which rested along the Red Sea, it took the average merchant five days to reach the capital city in the southwest. Adulis was ideally located for sea trade not only with the Middle East, but as far away as India, China, and Italy.

The empire stretched across a vital trade route reaching from the Red Sea to the Nile and up toward the southern ports of Arabia. Like modern cities, historians believe its power and wealth came mainly from trade, not agriculture. Its territory was too vast for farming alone to support it. At its peak, some estimate that the capital city supported over 20,000 residents. While not a city by 21st-century standards, at the time it was one of the largest on earth.

Gold was mined in the southern and central regions, then transported to the coast, while elephants and rhinos were slaughtered for their ivory and their horns. These rare and expensive goods were traded for vast quantities of glass, wine, spices, and textiles from far-away countries. By the 3rd century C.E., Aksum was minting its own money. Only powerful countries produced their own currency—merchants using the money had to believe in its producer. For sixty years, Aksum's money resembled currency used by Rome and Athens. Then, around 330 C.E., its design changed. Aksum's money bore a new image: the Christian cross.

Ethiopians travel from all over the country to celebrate Genna (Christmas) in Lalibela—a town modeled after Jerusalem.

A Christian Empire

In modern Ethiopia, Christmas comes late but services start early. Although the Orthodox Tewahedo Church does not celebrate Christmas until January 7, church services begin at 4 a.m.! The early start allows the mainly rural congregants to worship and still have time to return to their fields. Farm animals don't take holidays.

A traveler from the United States could enjoy Christmas holidays, have a leisurely week, hit the after-holiday sales, and still reach Ethiopia in plenty of time to enjoy the festivities for a second time. The Ethiopian calendar is based on the Egyptian Coptic calendar. It currently runs more than seven years behind the Gregorian calendar used in the United States and most other countries around the world. Not only does Christmas come late in Ethiopia, but most other Christian holidays are also observed later there than they are anywhere else.

Christmas, called Genna, is a festive celebration. Services begin with priests leading a procession around the church. Conducted in Ge'ez, an ancient language reserved for church services, the ceremony lasts about three hours.

Besides long church services, many Ethiopians celebrate the holiday by traveling to Lalibela. This city is home to eleven churches and was designed to resemble the traditional holy city of Jerusalem.

The Christian religion has been a powerful force in Ethiopia. It is not just a part of life for many of its people, but for over 1,600 years it was a central aspect of its rulers' lives. Until the 300s C.E., Aksumite kings were considered the offspring of a powerful warrior God named

Mahren. That belief was altered in the years after the two survivors of a ship attack made their way to the Aksum shore.

Syrian boys, educated in "humane studies," were accompanying their uncle Meropius, a Christian merchant. Returning from India, their ship was attacked and Meropius was killed. The boys survived and, according to the Ethiopian Church's official doctrine, they were originally brought to the royal court as slaves. Over time, their unique talents were appreciated. One of them, named Frumentius, rose to become the king's trusted royal treasurer. After the death of Emperor Ella Amida, his widow asked Frumentius to remain as her advisor until her infant son could become emperor. Frumentius agreed.

In Ethiopia, Saint Frumentius is revered for spreading Christianity throughout the kingdom.

FYI FACT:

Ancient Ethiopians were polytheist—they believed in numerous Gods, similar to ancient Greeks, Romans, and many native American cultures. Other Ethiopians were animists—they believed in spirits that inhabited every living thing. Although most Ethiopians today practice Christianity or Islam, a small minority still practice ancient religions.

The former slave began expanding his contacts with Christian merchants who arrived in Aksum for trade. Traveling to Alexandria, he asked the Egyptian bishop to send a representative of the church to Aksum. But the bishop thought Frumentius was the best person to represent the church, and he sent him back to Ethiopia as a bishop.

For the previous few centuries, Christians had been widely persecuted. In places like Rome, hundreds were tortured and even killed. But by the 300s, even the Roman Emperor Constantine had converted to Christianity.

When Aksum's newly-crowned Emperor Ezana converted to Christianity, it opened trade routes and increased the empire's wealth. By 400 C.E., the empire was stable and rich, with the numbers of Christians and their places of worship growing every year. Just a few hundred miles to the north, however, a new religion called Islam would soon be born that would win just as many converts. Ethiopia was prosperous, its capital city one of the largest in the world. But just outside its borders, a new threat was developing.

Ethiopia was a natural ally of the eastern Roman Byzantine Empire in their wars against Persia. Aksum kings had led wars of expansion, invading weaker rivals and subjecting them to Aksum rule. At its beginnings, the country's borders barely covered what is now northern Ethiopia. By 500 C.E., the country's territory had drastically expanded to include much of present-day Yemen, Eritrea, and Eastern Sudan.

The country's first openly religious conflict occurred around 520 C.E., when Aksum King Kaleb commanded a flotilla of ships attacking nearby Himyar, in modern-day Yemen. The Jewish Himyarite King Yusuf Asar Yathae had slaughtered the Christian residents of his country, and Kaleb believed he must be punished. Ethiopia won that

The Aksum Empire is known for the giant stelae (obelisks) that it left behind.

42

battle, bringing Himyar under its rule. But the expansive empire had a large border to defend and it was a Christian nation surrounded by others embracing a new religion. Its days of victory were numbered.

To the north, a prophet was busy converting. In 570 C.E., the same year Kaleb's general Abraha was defeated in a battle in Mecca, Muhammad was born. A trader by profession, he is considered by Muslims to be the last prophet—following Abraham, Moses, Jesus, and others. By 610 C.E., he was leading others to a new religion called Islam, but in Mecca they were attacked by the government. He urged his followers to seek asylum—protection from arrest—in Aksum.

These refugees were well received. The Ethiopian king listened to the teachings of Muhammad, and embraced Islam. Indeed, Muslim tradition holds that the king actually converted and he is referred to by his Islamic name—Ahmad al-Najashi. Muhammad for his part commanded his followers not to wage war with the country.

Despite this, Ethiopia had its challenges. In 570 C.E., General Abraha was overthrown in Himyar as the country achieved independence. Across the Red Sea in Africa, the conquered territories of Agaw and Beja attacked their client kings—local rulers who reported to the king.

With surrounding North Africa and the Middle East under Muslim control, the Aksumites found themselves in religious disputes with their trading partners. As they attacked Muslim cities, Muslims responded by attacking the Aksum port city of Adulis in 710. The trade that was vital to Ethiopia's power was all but eliminated.

Eventually the once-powerful empire of Aksum faded. Indeed, from 800 to 1100 C.E., so little is known about the country that the period is called "Ethiopia's Dark Ages."

FYI FACT:

Around 970 C.E., a female warrior named Gudit led an invasion of Aksum. Her army destroyed numerous churches and killed everyone they encountered.

Lalibela, the last Zagwe emperor, had eleven churches constructed from volcanic rock. The Church of St. George, shown here, was the last to be built and is also the most famous.

A Light in the Dark

"Encompassed on all sides by the enemies of their religion, the [E]thiopians slept near a thousand years, forgetful of the world, by whom they were forgotten," wrote Edward Gibbon in his classic book, *History of the Decline and Fall of the Roman Empire*.[1] Around 1137 C.E., a new kingdom arose. It probably originated within the Cushitic-speaking Agaw people, who had previously been ruled by the Aksumite kings. Known as the Zagwe dynasty, its people constructed churches which have outlasted its brief reign by nearly 1,000 years.

In the capital city of Roha, the last Zagwe emperor, Lalibela, constructed eleven of these churches "hewn directly out of the solid red volcanic rock on which they stand," describes writer Carol Beck-with. "Close examination is required before the full extent of this achievement can be appreciated: some of the churches lie almost completely concealed within deep trenches, while others hide in the open mouths of quarried caves."[2]

Modeled after Jerusalem, the town was renamed Lalibela in his honor. Today it is visited by many Orthodox Christians on Christmas Day.

The churches lasted. The empire disintegrated. Ethiopians expected their kings to be able to trace their lineage or descent from a common ancestor. That ancestor was Menelik I, the son of King Solomon and the Queen of Sheba. When a local chieftain named Yekuno Amlak revolted, he claimed to be related to the last Ethiopian king in the Aksum Empire. Like all of the kings in that empire, he was considered to be directly related to Menelik I. In 1270, Amlak overthrew the last Zagwe emperor and took over. His rule marked the beginning of an empire that would endure for over 700 years.

It was called the Solomonic Restoration. From its beginnings in 1270 until about 1600, the era was considered medieval—neither ancient nor modern. A campaign of conquest by Emperor Amda Tseyon in the 1300s expanded the empire's territory. The expansion continued for decades—until the independent kingdom of Gojjam, coastal Eritrea, and Damot to the south were all absorbed by Ethiopia.

Once-Muslim states were also added in the 15th century as Emperor Zara Ya'qob ruthlessly persecuted those who would not convert to Christianity much as the Spanish Inquisitors did in Europe. Indeed, by the late 1400s and early 1500s, Ethiopia's ties to Europe became more important as the country became increasingly isolated in a region dominated by Islam.

In 1520, the Portuguese established a mission in Ethiopia. And they would be needed when Adal leader Ahmad ibn Ibrihim al-Ghazi led Muslims in a holy war, or jihad, against Christian Ethiopia. After suffering several defeats, the Ethiopians enlisted the help of the Portuguese and were finally victorious over the Adal troops by 1559. But this would not be the end of Ethiopia's religious conflicts.

In the 16th century, the Cushitic-speaking Oromo represented a threat to the Christian state in the north and central regions of present-day Ethiopia. Many Oromo were Muslim. Wars between Christians

FYI FACT:

Across Europe, soldiers returning from Crusades in the Middle East told of a wealthy and powerful Christian priest and king. His name was Prester John, and for decades European explorers sought him out with little success. In pursuing their dreams of controlling trade from Africa and the Far East, European forces sought the ideal Christian ally. The Portuguese expedition to Ethiopia in 1487 didn't find Prester John, but it did find an ally in Ethiopia against Muslim-dominated East Africa.

During the Crusades, violent battles had devastating effects. Francesco Hayez's painting, *The Seventh Crusade Against Jerusalem*, depicts the aftermath of one such battle.

and Muslims had already been occurring for hundreds of years, including the Crusades where Christian nations attacked Muslim ones in hopes of taking over areas of religious significance.

The Oromo newcomers fought battles against the Ethiopian Empire. They attacked and settled further and further north, eventually reaching the Christian-dominated Central Highlands area of Ethiopia. Conflicts between the Oromo and the Ethiopians continued for hundreds of years.

In the 1600s, a new religious conflict began, not between Muslims and Christians, but between two groups of Christians. Across Africa, Catholic missionaries were converting native tribes. Ethiopian Emperor Za Dengel even converted to Catholicism. By doing this, he cut ties with the Egyptian Coptic Orthodox Church that administered the churches in Ethiopia. In 1604, Za Dengel was assassinated; in the 1630s Emperor Fasiladas kicked the Jesuit Catholic missionaries out of Ethiopia and removed any sign of Catholicism from the churches.

During the Gondar Period, Ethiopian royalty constructed elaborate castles, including the Palace of Fasiladas. Today, this restored castle is a popular tourist attraction.

Ethiopia became isolated. In 1636, Fasiladas moved the capital to Gondar, marking the beginning of what some call the Gondar Period. During this time, emperors spent most of their time living in tents, conducting military campaigns of expansion. When they weren't so occupied, they lived in stone castles in Gondar, just north of Lake Tana. These castles still remain, although many are crumbling. Reaching one means crossing a 16th-century arched stone bridge; others offer spectacular views of the city.

The empire itself was not as well constructed. In the 1700s, at least three emperors were killed; others died under suspicious circumstances. Through the 1850s, regional lords controlled the Ethiopian Empire. The kings themselves were so poor they died without decent burials as their castles fell into disrepair. It was a bad time to be weak. Europe was actively colonizing parts of Africa, taking over its land and exporting everything from ivory to coffee. France, Britain, and Italy were increasingly interested in profiting from Ethiopia's resources.

Tewodros II

Emperor Tewodros II eliminated rivals to rule over a stronger, united Ethiopia. He was also the first emperor in Ethiopia to work to modernize his country. Although he committed suicide in 1868 after losing a battle with the British, the emperors that followed continued to work to improve the country. In 1889, Emperor Menelik II encouraged the development of railways, banks, hospitals, and modern plumbing, and moved the capital to Addis Ababa ("The New Flower").

In the same year, he signed a treaty with Italy. There were two versions of this treaty, one written in Italian, the other in Amharic. The Amharic treaty gave the Italians control of Eritrea in exchange for weapons and money. The Italian version, which Menelik II could not read, made all of Ethiopia an Italian protectorate. When he realized what the Italians had done, he declared the treaty invalid. Italian forces invaded Ethiopia in 1895, but were defeated the next year by natives who banded together to preserve their country's independence. Italy's withdrawal from Ethiopia, however, did not change their interest in the nation.

During Italian occupation, the British assisted the Ethiopians in maintaining their independence. Even very young Ethiopians, including this fourteen-year-old boy, fought alongside British troops.

Return of
the Empire

For Emperor Haile Selassie, 1935 was the year everything changed. Previously known as Ras ("Duke") Tafari Makonnen, he was crowned emperor in 1930. Like his predecessors, Selassie worked hard to modernize his country and make it one of the world's great powers. He drafted a constitution which brought Ethiopia closer to democracy. His plans were interrupted when Italy invaded his country five years after he was crowned emperor.

Italian forces captured Addis Ababa in 1936, three years before the start of World War II. Led by dictator Benito Mussolini, Italy, like its allies, sought to expand its territory. Ethiopia, Eritrea, and Somalia became Italian East Africa. Selassie fled for his life, and petitioned for assistance from the League of Nations to defend Ethiopia's freedom.

As World War II gained momentum, Italy and Japan joined Nazi Germany to form the Axis powers, while the United States, France, and Britain came together with the Union of Soviet Socialist Republics to form the Allies. Fighting against invading Italy, Ethiopia naturally gained the sympathy of the Allied countries. British forces came to the aid of the Ethiopian military and finally defeated the Italians in 1941. Selassie returned a hero.

For over three decades, the reign of Emperor Selassie was marked by achievement and tragedy. He worked hard to ally his country with the United States and other western countries. Addis Ababa was chosen as the headquarters for both the United Nations Economic Commission for Africa and the Organization of African Unity. This helped the country to gain visibility and respect; after annexing Eritrea the country had a seaport as well.

Modernizing industry during Selassie's reign increased exports of crops like coffee and manufactured goods like footwear. The money earned from the exports allowed his government to build more roads and expand urban areas. But the progress came at a cost.

Used both for buildings and to heat homes, evergreen and juniper trees were cut down at an alarming rate. There is no consensus on how much of Ethiopia was covered in forests throughout history. But is generally agreed that the 14 percent of forest cover that remained in 1990 represented a significant loss of woodlands.

Although agriculture was producing a great deal of revenue, those profits were shared mainly by wealthy landowners. In 1958 and again in 1966, the country was gripped by famine. In 1973, when as many as 80,000 people starved to death in the Wollo Province, political unrest ensued among people who felt that Selassie wasn't doing enough to help.

Taking advantage of the situation, members of the military overthrew the empire. The group had Marxist ideals—they believed that no one should own land, that it should be distributed equally. This new regime, called the Dergue, seized large plantations and divided them up among the poor. They also executed sixty former leaders, including Selassie, along with thousands who opposed their rule.

The new regime failed far worse than the one that had preceded it. Its leader, General Tefari Benti, was killed in 1977 and replaced by Colonel Mengistu Haile Mariam. Farmers had only small lots of land, and since they were forced to sell their crops at low, government-set prices, they had little incentive to work. In the early 1980s, a series of

FYI FACT:

Haile Selassie's birth name inspired the Rastafari movement, a religion which was born in Jamaica. Rastas believe that Selassie was the reincarnation of Jesus, and study the teachings of the *Kebra Nagast.*

Images of famine, like this one of a starving Ethiopian family, prompted people around the world to give money to provide food aid.

droughts made conditions even worse. By 1984, hundreds of thousands, even millions of people were at risk of starvation. The world responded with an outpouring of money and food supplies.

As author John Reader notes, the efforts did little to help the starving. He blames "...the Mengistu government, which worked to ensure the world's humanitarian effort actually prolonged the suffering more than alleviated it. In Tigray in particular, aid supplies fed soldiers and not rural people. Overall the relief program helped to keep Mengistu in power longer."[1]

While the Mengistu regime survived the famine, it wasn't for long. Battles with Eritreans fighting for their independence weakened the Ethiopian military. Finally, in 1991 the Ethiopian People's Revolutionary Democratic Front captured the capital. Mengistu left the country. In 2006, he was convicted of genocide—mass killings—and later sentenced to death. Despite this, he currently lives in Zimbabwe under the protection of President Robert Mugabe.

The new government began democratic reforms, including a new constitution which gave more power to regional states than to the central government. There have been a number of challenges since. In 1993, Eritrea officially gained independence and Ethiopia lost its only seaport. Elections in 2010 gave the Ethiopian People's Revolutionary Democratic Front a majority in parliament and Prime Minister Meles Zenawi a fourth term. Observers from the European Union and the United States said the vote fell short of international standards.

On August 20, 2012, Prime Minister Zenawi died of an infection following brain surgery in a Belgian hospital. Hailemariam Desalegn, the deputy prime minister and minister of foreign affairs became acting prime minister. He was officially sworn in on September 21.

Economically, the country faces numerous obstacles. Two-thirds of the adult population isn't able to read or write. Famine and overpopulation are ongoing concerns. In 2004, the government began moving millions of people out of the Central Highlands where the food and water supply is not sufficient to sustain its population.

Today almost 80 percent of Ethiopians make their living by farming. Although farms in the United States rely on advanced machinery including diesel-powered plows, in Ethiopia most rural farms still use the oxen-powered maresha.

Dr. Eleni Gabre-Madhin is one woman who is working to improve Ethiopia's agriculture-based economy. She was born in Addis Ababa, but as the daughter of a United Nations official, she grew up living in several other African countries and the United States. With a PhD in Applied Economics from Stanford University, Gabre-Madhin went on

A modern warrior in the fight against hunger, Dr. Eleni Gabre-Madhin has used her Stanford doctorate and Ethiopian heritage to find ways to help the country's farmers earn more money and produce more food.

to work for the World Bank and the United Nations. With her job at the International Food Policy Research Institute, she moved back to Ethiopia in 2004 to help create policies to combat famine. She believes that if farmers can earn enough money from their crops, they will be more motivated to work. She developed the Ethiopia Commodity Exchange to ensure that trade in the country was efficient and modern. For her efforts, Gabre-Madhin was named Ethiopian Person of the Year in 2010, and in 2012 she was awarded the Yara Prize for work in African agriculture and food availability.

Despite Ethiopia's challenges, urban areas have grown more modern. The government has devoted increasing resources to improving cell phone service and internet connections in recent years. Although many Ethiopians still face hunger today, the country's resources and its history of enduring offer hope for the future.

Chickpea Wat

Wat is the national dish of Ethiopia. This stew can be a bit spicy for foreigners. The recipe below is both vegetarian and a little milder than the original.
Note: To cut down further on the spiciness, use less cayenne pepper.
Have an adult help with heating the oil and cutting vegetables!

Prep Time: 15 minutes
Total Time: 1 hour

This recipe makes enough for six people.

Ingredients:

2   tbsp extra virgin olive oil
1   large red onion, finely chopped
2   carrots, finely chopped
1   potato, peeled and chopped
½   tsp cayenne pepper
½   tsp paprika
½   tsp ginger
½   tsp salt
½   tsp black pepper
¼   tsp cumin
¼   tsp cardamom
1   tbsp tomato paste
1   c chickpeas (garbanzo beans)—if using canned chickpeas, drain and rinse them before using; if using dry chickpeas, cook them according to package directions before using
1½ c water
1   c frozen peas, thawed

Directions:

1. Place a large pot over medium heat, and add the oil.
2. Once the oil is heated, add the onion, cover the pot, and allow it to cook for about 5 minutes, or until the onion is soft.
3. Add the potato and carrots to the pot, replace the cover, and allow to cook for 10 minutes more.
4. Stir cayenne, paprika, ginger, salt, pepper, cumin, cardamom, and tomato paste into the pot. Add water and chickpeas, and bring the stew to a boil.
5. Turn the heat to low, and cover the pot. Allow the stew to simmer, and be sure to check regularly and add water if needed.
6. After about 20 minutes, check the taste of the stew, and add seasonings if needed. Add in the green peas and cover the pot again.
7. Continue simmering until vegetables are tender and the flavor is developed, about 30 minutes.

Ethiopian Art

Painting is a big part of traditional Ethiopian life, from the body painting of the Mursi people to the decorations found in churches. Art does not have to be complicated. Traditional Ethiopian art often has strong geometric patterns or shapes. These can be reproduced by using homemade stamps.

Supplies:
Paper
Paint
Brush
Markers
Knife
Potato, banana, pencil eraser, sponge, or any other object that can be used as a stamp

1. Cover your work surface with newspapers.
2. Create your stamps from household objects. You can create shapes with objects like potatoes, bananas, or sponges. Using markers, you can draw the shapes you'd like, and ask an adult to cut the shapes with the knife.
3. Dip one end of your stamp in the paint, or use the paint brush to apply it. Then press the painted end against the paper. You can make a continuous pattern or a more abstract design. Use the photos of the Mursi people's body art to inspire your work!

B.C.E.

ca. 4,400,000 Hominids—the ancestors of human beings—live in parts of the Great Rift Valley stretching from the Afar Depression in the northeast to the Omo Valley in the southwest.

ca. 2,500,000 Stone tools are first used.

ca. 7000 The region's population grows as animals like cattle, goats, and sheep are raised.

ca. 5000 Constant droughts produced by climate change drive farmers and herders from the plains and into the highlands.

ca. 3000 Some thirty-six different crops are cultivated in Ethiopia.

ca. 2500 Egyptians begin trading with the region known as Punt, in present-day Ethiopia.

ca. 1000 According to legend, King Solomon meets with Ethiopia's Queen of Sheba; they later have a son named Menelik who becomes Ethiopia's first Emperor.

800 to 500 In the highlands of what is now Eritrea and Tigray, people begin to speak and write in the Ge'ez language and script, influenced by South Arabian writing.

ca. 400 The Kingdom of Aksum arises.

C.E.

ca. 77 Pliny the Elder describes Aksum as an important trader of ivory, rhino horn, hippo hides, and slaves.

ca. 300 First use of the word "Ethiopia" to describe the country; the word is Greek for "burned faces."

330 After converting to Christianity, King Ezana declares it the state religion.

615 Muhammad tells a group of his Muslim followers to travel to Aksum to escape persecution.

970 Aksum is invaded by a female warrior named Gudit and her army.

1137 Beginning of the Zagwe dynasty.

ca. 1190 Lalibela is constructed, modeled after the holy city of Jerusalem.

1270 The last Zagwe emperor is overthrown, beginning the period known as the Solomonic Restoration.

1487 The Portuguese travel to Ethiopia in search of Prester John, a legendary Christian king.

1500-1600	Cushitic-speaking Somalis known as Oromo migrate to Ethiopia from the southern regions. They eventually spread throughout much of the country making up one-third of its population.
1529	Ahmad ibn Ibrihim al-Ghazi leads his Muslim Adal troops against Christian Ethiopia, beginning a holy war that would last for several decades.
1604	After converting to Catholicism, Emperor Za Dengel is assassinated.
1636	The Ethiopian capital is moved to Gondar.
1889	Addis Ababa becomes Ethiopia's capital; Emperor Menelik II signs a treaty with Italy giving the Italians control of Eritrea.
1895-1896	Italy invades Ethiopia; the Italian Army is defeated.
1930	Ras Tafari Makonnen is crowned emperor—takes name Emperor Haile Selassie I.
1935	Italy invades Ethiopia.
1941	The Italians are defeated by Ethiopian and British forces.
1962	Eritrea is annexed by Haile Selassie.
1973	Tens of thousands die of starvation in the Wollo Province.
1974	Selassie is overthrown by a military coup led by General Tefari Benti.
1977	Benti is killed and replaced by Mengistu Haile Mariam.
1984-1985	The worst famine in ten years kills hundreds of thousands of people; western countries provide tens of millions of dollars in aid, but much of it is taken by the military.
1991	Mengistu Haile Mariam flees the country after the Ethiopian People's Revolutionary Democratic Front seizes Addis Ababa.
1995	Ethiopia is divided into regions based upon each area's dominant ethnic group.
2010	Prime Minister Meles Zenawi wins a fourth term—opponents and outside observers claim the election was unfair.
2012	Zenawi dies of complications from brain surgery; he is succeeded by Hailemariam Desalegn.

Chapter 1. An Isolated World
1. John Reader, *Africa* (Washington, D.C.: National Geographic Society, 2001), p. 131.
2. Ibid., p. 131.
3. Ibid., p. 136.

Chapter 2. Beginnings
1. Stuart Munro-Hay, *Ethiopia, the Unknown Land* (New York: I.B. Tauris & Co Ltd., 2002), p. 17.
2. Pallab Ghosh, BBC News, "Ethiopia's Pride in 'Lucy' Find," September 20, 2006. http://news.bbc.co.uk/2/hi/science/nature/5364630.stm

Chapter 3. Culture
1. Hans W. Silvester, *Natural Fashion: Tribal Decoration From Africa* (London: Thames & Hudson, 2009), p. 3.

Chapter 4. On the Table
1. John Bolton, The Salt Lake Roasting Co., "Travel Journal—Ethiopia." http://user.xmission.com/~slrc/ethiopia-travel.html
2. John Reader, *Africa* (Washington, D.C.: National Geographic Society, 2001), p. 138.
3. UN Population Division/DESA, "Ethiopian Population Triples By 2050 Says US Census Bureau," Ayyaantuu News Online. http://ayyaantuu.com/horn-of-africa-news/ethiopia/ethiopian-population-doubles-by-2050/

Chapter 5. Trades
1. Alex Shoumatoff, *Vanity Fair,* "Agony and Ivory," August 2011, p. 122.
2. *Holy Bible New American Standard Version,* (La Habra, CA: The Lockman Foundation, 1995), p. 258.
3. John Reader, *Africa* (Washington, D.C.: National Geographic Society, 2001), p. 138.

Chapter 7. A Light in the Dark
1. Edward Gibbon, *History of the Decline and Fall of the Roman Empire,* Volume 4 (Philadelphia: J. B. Lippincott & Co., 1875), p. 563.
2. Carol Beckwith, Angela Fisher, and Graham Hancock, *African Ark* (New York: Harry N. Abrams, 1990), p. 14.

Chapter 8. Return of the Empire
1. John Reader, *Africa* (Washington, D.C.: National Geographic Society, 2001), p. 155.

FURTHER READING

Books

Bellward, Stacy. *Ethiopian Voices: Tsion's Life*. Minneapolis, Minn.: Amharic Kids, 2008.

Englar, Mary. *Ethiopia: A Question and Answer Book*. Mankato, Minn.: Capstone Press, 2006.

Gish, Steven. *Cultures of the World: Ethiopia*. Tarrytown, NY: Marshall Cavendish Benchmark, 2007.

Heinrichs, Ann. *Ethiopia*. New York: Children's Press, 2007.

Zuehlke, Jeffrey. *Ethiopia in Pictures*. Minneapolis: Lerner Publications Co., 2005.

On the Internet

Archaeologyinfo.com, "Homo sapiens"
    http://archaeologyinfo.com/homo-sapiens/

BBC News: *Africa,* "Ethiopia Profile"
    http://news.bbc.co.uk/2/hi/africa/country_profiles/1072164.stm

Ethiopian Treasures, "Culture"
    http://www.ethiopiantreasures.co.uk/pages/culture.htm

Link Ethiopia, "Guide to Ethiopia"
    http://www.linkethiopia.org/guide-to-ethiopia/

National Geographic, "Ethiopia"
    http://travel.nationalgeographic.com/travel/countries/ethiopia-guide/?source=A-to-Z

Smithsonian National Museum of Natural History: *What Does it Mean to be Human?,*
    "Australopithecus afarensis"
    http://humanorigins.si.edu/evidence/human-fossils/species/australopithecus-afarensis

U.S. Department of State, "Ethiopia"
    http://www.state.gov/p/af/ci/et/

World Guides, "Ethiopia Museums and Art Galleries"
    http://www.ethiopia.world-guides.com/ethiopia_museums.html

WORKS CONSULTED

Anthro4n6: "Australopithecus afarenis (Lucy)." http://www.anthro4n6.net/lucy/

Archaeologyinfo.com, "Australopithecus afarensis." http://archaeologyinfo.com/australopithecus-afarensis/

Beckwith, Carol, Angela Fisher, and Graham Hancock. *African Ark*. New York: Harry N. Abrams, 1990.

Bolton, John. "Travel Journal—Ethiopia." The Salt Lake Roasting Co. http://user.xmission.com/~slrc/ethiopia-travel.html

Cycon, Dean. Javatrekker: *Dispatches From the World of Fair Trade Coffee*. White River Junction, Vermont: Chelsea Green Publishing Company, 2007.

Gabre-Madhin, Eleni Zaude. "Ethiopia—This is My Ethiopian Story." Nazret.com, August 11, 2009.
    http://nazret.com/blog/index.php/2009/08/11/ethiopia_this_is_my_ethiopian_story_by_e

Ghosh, Pallab. "Ethiopia's Pride in 'Lucy' Find." BBC News, September 20, 2006. http://news.bbc.co.uk/2/hi/science/nature/5364630.stm

Gibbon, Edward. *History of the Decline and Fall of the Roman Empire*. Volume 4. Philadelphia: J. B. Lippincott & Co., 1875.

Greene, Melissa Fay. *There is No Me Without You*. New York: Bloomsbury USA, 2006.

Gruber, Ruth. *Rescue: The Exodus of the Ethiopian Jews*. New York: Athenuem, 1987.

Holy Bible New American Standard Version. La Habra, CA: The Lockman Foundation, 1995.

Marathonguide.com: "All Time Best Men's Marathon Times." http://www.marathonguide.com/history/records/alltimelist.cfm?Gen=M&Sort=Country

Marcus, Harold G. *A History of Ethiopia*. Berkeley: University of California Press, 1994.

Munro-Hay, Stuart. *Ethiopia, the Unknown Land*. London: I.B. Tauris & Co Ltd., 2002.

Reader, John. *Africa*. Washington, D.C.: National Geographic Society, 2001.

Robinson, Simon. "Abebe Bikila: Barefoot in Rome." *Time,* August 6, 2008.

Schoenherr, Neil. "Humans Evolved to Be Peaceful, Cooperative And Social Animals, Not Predators." Medical News Today, February 20, 2006. http://www.medicalnewstoday.com/releases/38011.php

Shoumatoff, Alex. "Agony and Ivory." *Vanity Fair,* August 2011. p. 122.

Silvester, Hans W. *Natural Fashion: Tribal Decoration From Africa.* London: Thames & Hudson, 2009.

TED, "Speakers Eleni Gabre-Madhin: Economist." http://www.ted.com/speakers/eleni_gabre_madhin.html

Thurow, Roger, and Scott Kilman. *Enough: Why the World's Poorest Starve in an Age of Plenty.* New York: PublicAffairs, 2009.

UN Population Division/DESA. "Ethiopian Population Triples by 2050 Says US Census Bureau." Ayyaantuu News Online. http://ayyaantuu.com/horn-of-africa-news/ethiopia/ethiopian-population-doubles-by-2050/

Visonà, Monica Blackmun. *A History of Art in Africa.* New York: Harry N. Abrams, 2001.

GLOSSARY

evolve (ee-VOLV): To change over a period of time as an adaptation to the environment.

genetics (juh-NET-iks): The study of how physical traits are passed from one generation to the next.

fossil (FAHS-uhll): The remains or impression of a living creature preserved in the earth's crust.

hominid (HAH-muh-nid): The classification of primates that stand and move on two feet, such as humans, gorillas, and chimpanzees.

nomad (NOH-mad): A person with no fixed home who moves from place to place.

reincarnation (ree-in-kar-NAY-shun): The rebirth of a soul into a new body.

republic (ree-PUB-lik): Government whose chief of state is not a monarch; the greatest power rests with its citizens who vote for their representatives.

retinue (RET-n-yoo): A group of people that accompanies an important person such as a king or queen.

savanna (suh-VAN-uh): Tropical or subtropical grasslands with few trees.

Born in Boston, Massachusetts, John Bankston began writing articles while still a teenager. Since then, over 200 of his articles have been published in magazines and newspapers across the country, including travel articles in *The Tallahassee Democrat, The Orlando Sentinel,* and *The Tallahassean.* He is the author of over sixty biographies for young adults, including works on Alexander the Great, scientist Stephen Hawking, author F. Scott Fitzgerald and actor Jodi Foster. At sixteen he enjoyed his first experience with overseas adventure, visiting Italy for two weeks with his sophomore Latin class. He currently lives in Newport Beach, California where the January temperature rarely dips below 40 degrees Fahrenheit and the August highs top 75 degrees.